SORRY WHATTTTTT???????

JYOTI

XpressPublishing
An imprint of Notion Press

No.8, 3rd Cross Street,CIT Colony,
Mylapore, Chennai, Tamil Nadu-600004

ISBN 978-1-64892-314-2

Contents

Acknowledgements

Thanking the supreme power of the universe for getting me started here. The idea of this book came during quarantine.Ya! one of the time when corona hit and got pandemic,this book is also a result of many circumstances which I got through my life.But one of the most lovely person of my life motivated me to get it published and I, from the bottom of my heart want to thank him(no, I ain't mentioning his name).
I almost quit writing but then one day, I felt that modern, independent women needs to be praised for what they are because though they soare high, society and typical stereotypes try to pull them down and I think one person can motivate the other. So,here I am.
To my beloved father in heaven, I thank you for bestowing your blessings onto me. Standing there with me, throughout my ups and downs I'm thankful to my family members and each and everyone of them for playing various roles in my life(esp.maternal grandparents, maternal aunts and my mom).
My best friends are also to be grateful for keeping me right on my track,when I tend to lost it and get low. To my school teachers,nuturing me with best values which I realised when I entered the real world and trust me, it's more valuable than having those highest scoring degrees, thank you.To few of the members of my fitness studio, guiding me when I was away from my family, bringing gifts with included some of the life changing books, thank you everyone for this bond.
Last but not the least, notion press publishing, thank you.

SORRY, WHATTTTT????

What to do & what not to do & how to...-THAT'S WHAT A
MODERN, INDEPENDENT WOMAN ENCOUNTERS
DAILY (KICKING OFF THE STEREOTYPES).

We don't care what they(nosy people)say ,we accept what
we are because that is who we are.

No matter how advanced is this contemporary era getting, how much we(modern, independent women)are prospering and succeeding, at some point we will encounter some of the not so needed advice from anyone yet everyone.

(Shuruwaat se shuru karein toh) If we start from the very beginning; Oh look, it's a girl, paraya dhan hai,padh likh k chali jaegi sasuraal, anyways congratulations on your baby girl….SORRY WHATTTTT????…. And here her future gets decided (& she glances with this only thought in her mind, "where the hell you guys came from?").

Undoubtedly, there are many families who are really beyond this stereotype and a girl is lucky if she is born there.

Along with the course of time, we all grow, and there starts a more tough world for all the modern, independent women.

While running late for her school, it was her maths (most terrifying) exam and as she rushed towards the altar, sound approaches,"beta bahar jao"; I told you already, not at the Time Of The Month, SORRY,WHATTTTT???.......

I think it's a biological phenomena.

Then she decided to focus on her exam rather this stereotype.

And here's more...she returned ,almost rocking her math exam, exhausted and was starving, game didn't end there and as she approaches towards the kitchen,"Pehele Nahalo, fir khana milega and how many times I have to tell you that you can not enter into the kitchen" and here she had to follow because she was starving .

So, what I think is, it's all the stereotypes which should be considered a little(nevermind) and what ones practical and real life requires should be aimed at, taking into consideration that periods are something that we are blessed into our physiology. So, C'mon....

Then what I say,a not so tailor-made perspective; "dress dekho uski, kal bhi crop-top tha, aaj sleeveless...koi sanskaar nahi hai", SORRY,WHATTTTT???....

Well, clothes doesn't define her character and dignity. She is free to wear every decent apparel she loves to and in which she is comfortable. There is another word termed as respect, well...that should be earned.

Why the hell nobody has an objection(stomach ache) when a man wears shorts in some park and runs???Why always women gets all the uncomfortable looks and comments from everyone?

And that's all what continues...

While deciding to go abroad for her higher education and to pursue her career, her parents seemed to be supportive enough and everything was running smooth until……(padoos ki aunty),

"Videsh jarahi hai? Ha sahi hai acchi job karegi toh accha ghar(in-laws) miljaega", SORRY,WHATTTTT???........

Is that how it ends? Is this the only thing left to get worried about? Can't she be ambitious? Ain't she allowed to dream? This is actually (one of) the most annoying thing a modern, independent woman's ears have to hear. Maybe she wants to make her parents proud and become their "so called SON by the society". But some typical and illogical minds would never understand the meaning and value of ambitions.

While life continues and she (modern, independent woman) chooses to be the man of her life, the boss of her life, she has to confront various situations while going through this phase but she does it anyway and does it in a commendable manner.

When her job phase starts, she experiences many sorts of odds and various inappropriate taunts. And that's here......

One of the contender, "kaafi asaan hoga aapke liye toh, after all you are a beautiful woman with this appealing dress. The boss here might have gone bananas over you, we don't have any chance left for this job, I guess".

SORRY,WHATTTTT???........ Well, God bless such teeny-tiny mindsets. She might have an edge over people like this contender because of her knowledge, skills and her personality which such small minds would never get and such things remain far from their senses.

So many modern, independent women comes face to face with such situations on a daily basis and trust me, not giving a damn is the best thing she can do (knowing she excels in her work and her skills).

One day, while returning late from work, she hears some whispering, "Ye konsa time hai bahar ghoomne ka, has she lost it? Who comes that late??"

SORRY,WHATTTTT???........ She would probably return when she is done with her work and she may have a collection of never ending files on some days in a month .Consequently, she runs late.But kya hai naa you guys would surely judge her and pass such cliche` remarks.

She accepts it in an unwavering manner because she is a self made person and she is independent, unlike you who are worthless and are way too nosy and are dependent on someone else for your living, for your all necessities, etc. and can't even raise your voice at being right or in making any decision .

Then one day, she was pondering over buying a mansion for herself. Unfortunately, her relatives planned to visit her that very day. Oh oh....

Relative, "Sb set hai, shadi kab karegi? Ab to umar(age) bhi horahi hai."

SORRY,WHATTTTT???.......Would somebody explain what was that about? Who made that book of golden rules? The information that justifies this "Umar statement",who wrote it? The society?????

What if she doesn't want to get married? What if she want to support many poor homeless children or some NGO running and supporting such cause?

What if she, after reading about or viewing all the extra-marital affairs gave up and plan to have a dog and a lovely house for herself?What if she plans to keep her only family member left, her sick old father with her and serve him and care for him till the end of the time? What if she aims at making her name successfully in FORBES 30 under 30????

Grow up people. Marriages are not the final or the only goal of many women out there.

Whilst everything goes hand in hand, flowing along with the course of time...questions starts to knock like, will you live all by your own in this mansion of yours?

Who will look onto all the finances and other made for man(according to the society) chores and errands of your house?

She (modern, independent woman) bravely says, she would.

She gets entitled to labels like being arrogant, selfish, outspoken, rebel... giving no damn to LOG KYA KAHENGE, hence breaking the stereotypes, she moves on in her life very confidently, setting an example for many the women out there who hesitate a lot in coming out of this web and those who are being crushed by imposition of other's beliefs on them.

Hence, she imparts courage to others to take a stand for themselves.

Once in her lifetime, she experiences a phase called, "To get or not to get married"?

She is way too independent and ambitious that she encounters this interrogative phase a lot and that's fair enough because she has become the man she needed, only love is to be found now.

But that may sound a lot to ask these days. As she owns a modern, independent image it gets a little,um.. a lot more tough.

She gets,

"Beta itne modern clothes humarey yaha nahin chalenge".

"Tattoo, OMG! another symbol of disrecpect and inappropriate thing for a girl".

"HELLO? GOOD MORNING?? What's that? Only touching feet is considerable here".

"Gym jana chorna hoga,ghar kaise dekhegi? How will you have babies if you get so slim??"

"Khana banana toh sikhaya hi hoga mummy ne". And such crap goes on.

SORRY,WHATTTTT??????...................

She owns a firm belief that respect is from within, one can't pretend it and neither can someone beg for respect.

And of course,

"Modern kapde, does those define me?" I will wear whatever I love to.

"Tattoo is not another thing to define my character, mom and dad bhi likha ho sakta hai yr tattoo mein". But I don't give a damn now.

"Hello, good morning, etc. might be her way to express respect and to greet everyone and why can't you allow your minds to accept it that she might not be comfortable in touching feet or that,she might not have this trend in her family. She is free to express in the way she likes."

"Gym, fitness is an imperative element of our lives. And she's a multi-tasker and can efficiently manage her work, her time and home concomitantly. So stop making it hard for her by being so negative and unsupportive".

And don't get me started on babies.

"I didn't opt for any hotel management course or for some home science class by my mother. She might have given me all the love she can and enriched me with other moral values. Especially, the one where I was being taught not to be JUDGEMENTAL."

Absolutely, this journey is very tough for a modern, independent woman.

But there comes a day, she acknowledges a man who ain't dominating like most of the men, who doesn't care if she wears a skirt or a suit, who doesn't bothers to ask if she can cook or not but believes that they would keep someone to assist her, who stands for her always, fighting all the odds together, who at no point in her life may judge her, who is way too far from body shaming, who knows she is a hero but he loves her in a way that only he wins her heart. Trust me, marry him whether you are at the age of 24,32 or 62 and that doesn't matter.

The story doesn't ends here because she is the same and she experiences all the comments and taunts on how she's dealing with her life now, managing everything in a balanced manner. She is her own hero but she finds a person who values her and loves her for what she is and on this one, she can rely completely.

Well, journey is really a lot controversial if you are a modern, independent woman in today's scenario.

Your rebel heart, your outstanding ideas, your style of working or hustling no less than a man , the statement of carrying your personality confidently apart from all those running conflicts and your no dependence nature. It actually kills all the stereotypes and scares all the misleading and dominating perspectives of many people out there. You own it all.

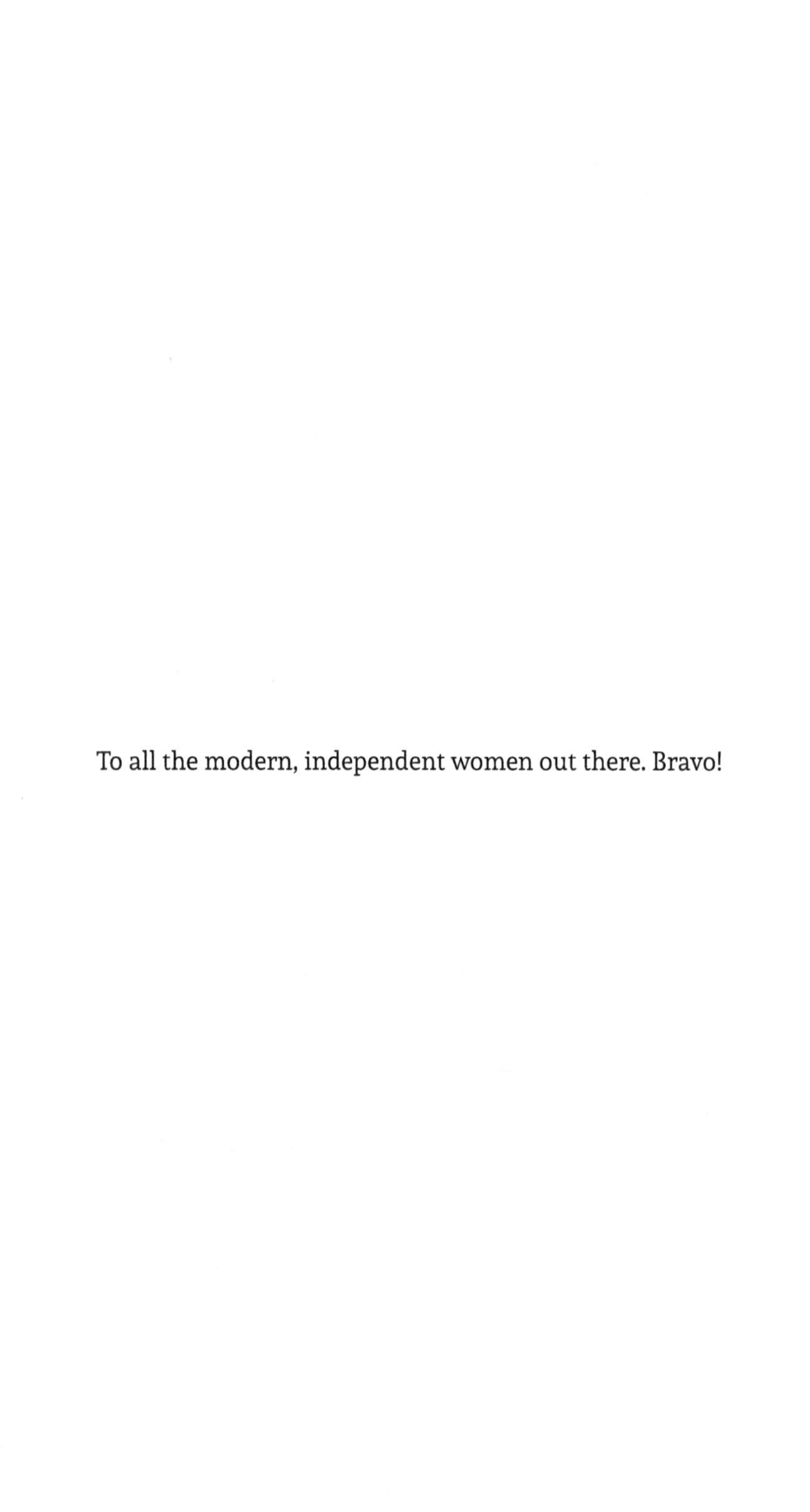

To all the modern, independent women out there. Bravo!